Marrisson Murilo De A. Farias
Ivanildo F. Araújo

Quality, implications and barriers in small companies

Marrisson Murilo De A. Farias
Ivanildo F. Araújo

Quality, implications and barriers in small companies

Understanding the challenges of new ventures

ScienciaScripts

Imprint

Any brand names and product names mentioned in this book are subject to trademark, brand or patent protection and are trademarks or registered trademarks of their respective holders. The use of brand names, product names, common names, trade names, product descriptions etc. even without a particular marking in this work is in no way to be construed to mean that such names may be regarded as unrestricted in respect of trademark and brand protection legislation and could thus be used by anyone.

Cover image: www.ingimage.com

This book is a translation from the original published under ISBN 978-613-9-65086-6.

Publisher:
Sciencia Scripts
is a trademark of
Dodo Books Indian Ocean Ltd. and OmniScriptum S.R.L publishing group

120 High Road, East Finchley, London, N2 9ED, United Kingdom
Str. Armeneasca 28/1, office 1, Chisinau MD-2012, Republic of Moldova, Europe
Printed at: see last page
ISBN: 978-620-7-84925-3

ACKNOWLEDGEMENTS

I thank the Creator Father for life, courage and protection. I'm grateful for another opportunity to be incarnate, enjoying new experiences and improving my intelligence and morals.

Thank you to my greatest example of a man, of honesty, morality and courage, who carried on his back the burden of responsibility for supporting and guiding a large family, who endured the sadness and worries that the world threw at him so as not to worry his children, who taught me about life and spared no effort to protect and encourage each of his children. I thank you, my father.

I would like to thank my greatest example of love, dedication, care and affection, the woman who wrapped me in love, protected me, guided me and nurtured me from the first day of my life. She who dedicates every day of her life to loving her children and grandchildren, who cares first and foremost about the well-being of others rather than her own. I thank you, my mother.

Thank you to my brothers, my first example of society, who encouraged me to understand the plurality of thoughts, the need to share, to understand, to unite for a happier life. Thank you for the fights, thank you for the complaints, thank you for the encouragement, the companionship and the protection.Thank you to my grandmother Severina, grandmother Guia, grandfather Orlando. Their love, their smiles and their grandmotherly joy will always remain in my heart.

I would like to thank my beloved Luana, who has accompanied me for seven years, strengthened me, sustained me and nurtured me with her unconditional love. Thank you for always guiding me, making me see the good side of life, for always encouraging me to go further, for all of which I am very grateful.

Thank you to my friends, who have always been willing to lend a hand to help me, who have been by my side in times of joy and sorrow. To you, my friends from Iowa, Mizzou, UFE, Taekwondo, or anywhere in the world, you have taught me the value of friendship.

Thank you to all the teachers in my life, the sum of your work is reflected in today's result, you transformed an illiterate child with no confidence into an engineer ready to take flight.

Finally, thank you all very much, I have the deepest sense of gratitude for all of you, because I wouldn't have been able to get where I am without you.

SUMMARY

This study aims to map the characteristics of small companies in order to identify the main implications and barriers inherent in the use of new quality philosophies and tools. In this way, the study focused on the characteristics that define small companies, identifying structural, economic and organisational aspects. It was identified that despite the notorious relevance of quality practices stemming from quality philosophies and tools, a small percentage of small companies used these methodologies. Thus, through bibliographical research and informal interviews and questionnaires with entrepreneurs from small companies, it was possible to indicate possible causes of barriers that prevent or hinder the implementation of new quality practices, as well as the consequences that these practices have brought to the companies that have applied them. By analysing case studies and the ISO 9001 standard, it was found that even philosophies and tools aimed at improving business quality have their negative points and limitations, which can diverge from the company's strategic planning, leading to possible losses. The study provides knowledge about the complex problem of implementing new quality programmes, as well as making it possible to develop new methodologies for applying changes, avoiding practices that could negatively influence managers' objectives.

Keywords: Quality philosophy and tools, Small businesses, Barriers, Implications, Implementation.

SUMMARY

CHAPTER 1

INTRODUCTION

Evolution brings progress to nature, humanity, thoughts and actions. Being on the fringes of evolution, not walking alongside progress is potentially dangerous, the consequences of remaining stagnant in time are high, so that it is not possible to adapt and survive in a new environment, the history of planet earth and humanity reveal this truth (DARWIN, 2003). In his theory on the origin of species, Charles Darwin showed humanity that living beings were constantly changing, adapting to their environment over the generations.

In a competitive environment, those who have advantages over their competitors are more likely to survive. In corporate environments, this reality can also be applied. Corporations compete with each other in an attempt to hold a larger share of the market (GHOBRIL; BENEDITTI; FRAGOSO, 2014). These market disputes enabled the development of production techniques and equipment, transforming skilled artisans into essential resources for groups or kingdoms. This development culminated in the first industrial revolution in the 17th century (LINS, 2000). The advent of the first steam engine enabled the emergence of automated machines, improving productivity and making mass production a reality.

As a result, techniques and equipment continued to develop, skilled craftsmen were replaced by machines operated by employees without many skills, following product quality standards. Thus, several mechanised companies emerged, making the environment even more competitive, as one company could now supply the demand of a large part of the market. Acquiring competitive advantages was essential for the company's survival, and various theories, methodologies, philosophies and quality tools have been developed over the centuries, driving the improvement of the production system and the product, maximising the company's productivity, generating higher profits and the appropriate use of scarce resources.

Within this context are small businesses, which, in a competitive environment, have to compete for a share of the market with large companies, win customers, offer more attractive products, have bargaining power, among other things that small businesses may have disadvantages in relation to larger companies. However, small businesses are essential organisations for a country's economy, and letting them compete with large companies without some advantages could be damaging for the country (SEBRAE, 2011). The Brazilian constitution, in its article 179, defines the state's responsibility to guarantee an environment favourable to the growth of micro and small enterprises (MSEs).

However, in order to guarantee the survival of small businesses, government incentives are not enough; small businesses need to be able to manage and improve their activities. Thus, quality tools and philosophies play a fundamental role in strengthening these businesses (SANTOS, 2006). Despite playing a fundamental role, a large proportion of small businesses, around 54 per cent, do not use innovation in their production system (SEBRAE, 2013).

In 2015, 581,469 MSEs went out of business, while according to SEBRAE, an average of 1.2 million businesses are created every year. And another study published by the IBGE in 2015 revealed that only 47.5 per cent of companies remained active three years after they were set up. These figures reveal the fragility of MSEs in Brazil, which have a high level of mortality, which consequently makes the country's economy fragile.

In this way, this research sought to survey the main barriers and consequences of using quality philosophies and tools in small companies, with the aim of anticipating possible problems in their application and making the use of quality practices more accessible, thus enabling small companies to become stronger.

The work is divided into five chapters, as described below. The first chapter presents the introduction to the research topic, the general and specific objectives, as well as the justification for the research. The second chapter deals with the theoretical basis on which the research is based in order to analyse the data collected, draw conclusions and make suggestions. The third chapter demonstrates the research methodology, showing the procedures that were carried out to obtain the data. The fourth chapter deals with the results and discussions of the research, showing the data collected and discussing possible causes and solutions to the problems observed. The last chapter contains the author's final considerations on the data obtained and analysed in relation to the second chapter.

1.1. Objective

1.1.1. General Objective

Carry out a survey of the main barriers and implications regarding the use of quality philosophies and tools in small companies.

1.1.2. Specific Objective

In order to fulfil the general objective, the following specific objectives were used:

- Carry out a detailed study of the economic and structural aspects of small companies, as well as a study of quality tools and philosophies in terms of their use and applicability;
- Analyse case studies available for consultation on the use of quality philosophies and tools;
- Comparing the editions of the ISO 9001 standard, identifying its limitations and negative points;
- Carry out interviews, assisted by a questionnaire, with entrepreneurs from small companies, with the aim of identifying the barriers and implications of using new quality philosophies and tools in their company.

1.2. Justification

In 2015, Brazil entered a serious economic crisis, its GDP shrank by 3.8 per cent (IBGE, 2016), the number of MSEs that closed down in 2015 grew by 298.61 per cent compared to the previous year, further aggravating the country's economic recession. Due to this fact, some questions arise, such as:

- Why are small businesses in Brazil more susceptible to market destabilisation if they receive greater tax incentives, interest and consultancy from the government, and are more flexible to change?
- Why is the number of companies that survive more than three years on the market so low?
- Do small businesses know about quality philosophies and tools?
- Do small businesses use these tools?

- Do small businesses benefit or suffer from applying these quality programmes?
- What barriers do small businesses face when implementing such quality programmes?

These questions involve various factors in their answers, making the answers complex. However, the fact is that MSEs are the first to feel the effects of economic imbalance, they are the first to close their doors in times of crisis. Companies can only achieve their goals if their internal environment is strengthened to the point where they are able to fulfil their planned objectives, because "business strategy will mobilise all available resources: financial, technological, human, directing them towards achieving long-term objectives, with the aim of increasing profitability" (PELISSARI, 2007, p168).

Thus, the high mortality rate of small companies in Brazil may be associated with the fragility of the internal environment. Therefore, these companies may not be investing in internal strengthening, or investing in the wrong way. As the aim of quality philosophies and tools is to strengthen the company's operations, it would be essential to use them to strengthen small companies internally.

A study is needed to verify the use of quality tools and philosophies, as well as a survey of the main barriers to the application of these quality practices. Understanding why small companies resist using new philosophies and tools in their operations is fundamental for their growth and strengthening. This research is therefore necessary to understand the implications and barriers present in small companies when using new quality philosophies and tools, in order to provide relevant data for further research, understanding for small business owners, and the creation of new methodologies for applying quality practices.

CHAPTER 2

THEORETICAL BACKGROUND

This chapter will present the characteristics that define small businesses, as well as the economic context to which they belong. The characteristics of quality tools and philosophies, their positive and negative points, as well as case studies demonstrating their applicability. The barriers that hinder the application of quality programmes, as well as the implications for the company of adopting quality practices.

2.1. Small businesses

2.1.1. Economy and Mortality

Small businesses play a fundamental role in the economy and in strengthening a country. In Brazil, small businesses (EPP) accounted for 16.3 per cent of all industries, 11.7 per cent of service providers and 9.8 per cent of the commercial sector in 2011 (SEBRAE, 2014).

In 2011, small businesses, together with micro-enterprises, accounted for 27 per cent of GDP (Gross Domestic Product), and in Paraíba they contributed 29.6 per cent of GDP.

In the state of Paraíba, according to the Brazilian Institute of Tax Planning (IBPT), there are 178,236 micro and small companies, of which 3,565 are small companies, which together collected R$ 749,175,306.32 in 2016 (data from 5 August 2016).

As it is one of the pillars of economic equilibrium, it is up to the government to incentivise micro and small businesses, according to article 179 of the 1988 federal constitution. In this way, the government can incentivise them with tax exemptions, low-interest bank loans, support for technological development, providing workplaces, among other initiatives. Graph 1 below shows that GDP growth is sensitive to changes in MSE mortality. In this way, the development of MSEs is essential for a country's economic balance and development.

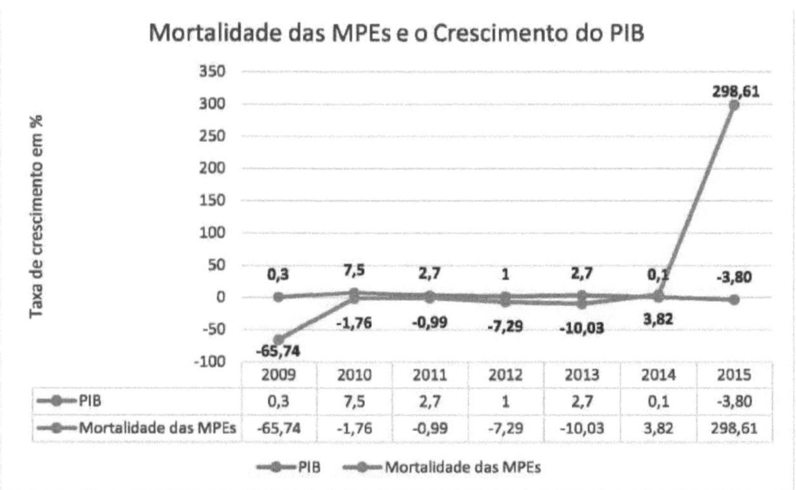

	2009	2010	2011	2012	2013	2014	2015
PIB	0,3	7,5	2,7	1	2,7	0,1	-3,80
Mortalidade das MPEs	-65,74	-1,76	-0,99	-7,29	-10,03	3,82	298,61

Graph 1: Relationship between MSE mortality and GDP growth
Sources: IBGE and IBPT (2016)

In order to achieve this, companies must gain competitive advantages that allow them to expand their activities, acquiring a larger market share and generating more wealth for both the organisation and the country. However, gaining a foothold in the market requires strategies that allow these companies to acquire a competitive advantage over others in the market. According to WRIGHT, KROLL AND PARNELL (2010, p. 25):

> "Strategic management consists of administrative decisions and actions that help ensure that the organisation formulates and maintains beneficial adaptations to its environment. Thus, it can be inferred that companies are influenced by their external environment, and must adapt to benefit from the opportunities observed."

In this sense, Wright, Kroll and Pamell also point out that strategic managers must evaluate their companies by deriving strengths and weaknesses, thus seeing opportunities and threats that influence their strategies. As a result, companies must be fully prepared to keep up with market developments and take advantage of growth opportunities.

However, the death rate of micro and small companies has been rising considerably in Brazil. The IBPT shows that the number of bankrupt MSEs, comparing the years 2014 and 2015, increased by around 300%, this increase meaning around 440 (four hundred and forty thousand) more MSEs closed their doors.

According to a study carried out by SEBRAE/MG in 2004 based on the spontaneous opinions of ex-entrepreneurs and active entrepreneurs, the main causes for the closure of their businesses are low sales, lack of capital and tax burdens. For those who remain active, they point to factors such as high tax burdens, lack of working capital and the economic recession as the main difficulties faced in keeping companies going.

The study carried out by SEBRAE/MG also asked which were the main factors favouring the survival of the enterprise, and in response there were three main factors, such as good knowledge of the market, a good sales strategy and the entrepreneur's creativity. Issues such as quality control, production management and reducing waste were not mentioned in the survey.

"Good management is a determining factor for the survival and success of all companies, especially small ones, and this consists of the ability to understand, direct and control their processes" (OLIVEIRA, 2006).

A study published by the Institute for Applied Economic Research (IPEA) in 2012 revealed that in 2009, in MSEs with more than 11 employees, only 3.9 per cent of workers had a university degree and 44.1 per cent had completed high school. This proportion rises when compared to employers, where 55.6 per cent have completed high school and 28.5 per cent have completed high school. These figures may reveal the fragility of MSEs, since having knowledge of the area in which they operate is not the only preponderant factor for a company's survival, but rather having a set of skills that make "good management" possible.

2.1.2. Structural characteristics

In Brazil, micro and small businesses are classified, for legal purposes, according to the Micro and Small Business Statute of 1999, which was revised in 2014 by the National Congress and sanctioned on 7 August 2014 through LC (Complementary Law) No. 147/2014 in its Chapter 2, Article 3. 3º , item I classifies a micro-enterprise as a business company, a simple company, an individual limited liability company and a legal entity that has annual gross revenue equal to or less than R\$ 360,000.00, and item II classifies a small business that, while not classified as a micro-enterprise, has annual gross revenue greater than R\$ 360,000.00 and equal to or less than R\$ 3,600,000.00.

However, other federal government bodies, such as SEBRAE and the BNDES (National Bank for Economic and Social Development), classify MSEs based on other indicators, such as the number of employees or gross annual operating revenue, as shown in Table 1 and 2.

Table 1: Criteria for classifying company size by: persons employed

	Number of employees	
Classification (size)	**Industry**	**Trade and Services**
Micro-enterprise	0a19	0a9
Small Business	20 a 99	10 a 49
Medium-sized companies	100 a 499	50 a 99
Large Company	Above 500	Above 100

Source: SEBRAE-2014

Table 2: Classification of company size adopted by the BNDES

Classification (size)	**Annual gross operating revenue**
Micro-enterprise	Less than R\$ 2.4 million
Small Business	Greater than 2.4 million and less than or equal to R\$ 16 million
Medium-sized companies	Greater than 16 million and less than or equal to R\$ 90 million

Medium-Large Company	Greater than 90 million and less than or equal to R$ 300 million
Large Company	Above R$ 300 million

Source: BNDES-2016

In addition to the small number of employees and revenue compared to large companies, small companies in Brazil have their own characteristics that are cited by various authors and researchers. According to Schell apud Oliveira (1995), small companies have the following characteristics.

- They have a simple organisational structure, with few hierarchical levels and a high concentration of authority;
- They occupy a defined space in their market;
- They have locational flexibility;
- They are more labour intensive;
- Properties and administration are highly correlated;
- Absolute predominance of national private capital.

Other authors, such as Rodrigues (2000), Gonsalvez and Koprowski (1995), and Moreira & Souza (2004), reinforce these characteristics and cite others, such as: the use of their own labour or that of family members; the owner's close relationship with employees, customers and suppliers; and difficulties in obtaining credit.

Albuquerque (2004) classifies the structure of small companies according to Table 1.

Table 1: Structural characteristics of small businesses

Features	Specificities
- Division of labour	• Few work units • Greater job scope for the management function • Minimal concern for job requirements
- Authority System	• Centralised authority • Wider range of control facilities • Little or no authority
- Form of communication	• Direct and informal contact with employees and external public • Predominance of downward communication

Small companies have greater structural flexibility than large companies. This flexibility comes from the ease of allocating resources, the simplicity of controlling the various variables and the low number of *stakeholders* (BOAS, A., 2006, p 27). In this way, small companies have fertile ground for process, product, organisational and marketing innovation.

A study published in 2013 by SEBRAE, which interviewed 2,326 entrepreneurs from all Brazilian states about their level of innovation, showed that 75.1% of these entrepreneurs had carried out some kind of innovation in their company. However, of those who gave an affirmative answer about innovation in their company, only 53.4% said they had carried out organisational or process innovations, the ones that came out on top in terms of innovation were in the product area, with 78.1%, and marketing, with 59.3%.

> "[...] innovations in process development, customer service, relationships with suppliers, the definition of the organisational structure, individual and group interactions within the organisation, the conception of the business and the treatment of environmental issues, as elements in which organisations considered to be innovative stand out" (SOUSA, 2006, p 16).

This data shows that small companies consider product or sales innovation to be the priority innovation, so they leave essential issues such as organisational innovations or strengthening themselves internally to take advantage of external opportunities to the background. As mentioned by Sousa, companies that are considered innovative invest in organisational and process innovation as essential to their growth. However, there are a number of barriers that make it impossible to implement new working methods, new organisational philosophies and the use of tools aimed at improving the productivity of organisations, leaving small companies stagnant in their market or leading to the bankruptcy of their businesses.

2.1.3. Small businesses in Paraíba

Since the beginning of the 19th century, Paraíba's economy has been characterised by agriculture, with the largest number of workers and population concentrated in rural areas. In 1990, with the opening up of trade and the restructuring of production that took place in Brazil, a series of changes were unleashed in Paraíba's economy (IPEA, 2012, p 36). Table 03 shows the sectoral composition of employment in 2002, 2005 and 2009.

Table 3 shows that the number of workers in the agricultural sector in Paraíba has fallen in recent years, according to the census. However, agriculture is still the sector that employs the most people in the state, generating around 364,080 jobs (PNAD, 2010). According to data from IPEA (2010) on the evolution of the share of agriculture in Paraíba's GDP between 1960 and 2007, the contribution of the agricultural sector fell from 56.8% to 5%. In contrast, industry's share of Paraíba's GDP rose from 9% to 20.1%, peaking in 2000 at 27.9%, and data from IBPT (2016) shows that the number of active MSEs jumped from 53,559 in 2007 to 179,056 in 2016.

Table 3: Sectoral share of employment - 2002-2009 in Paraíba

Sector	Years		
	2002	2005	2009
Agriculture	35,3%	32,2%	24,2%
Industry	9,9%	10,7%	11,5%
Construction	5,9%	4,2%	7,7%
Trade and Repair	14,4%	15,7%	16,2%
Accommodation and Food	2,8%	3,2%	3,7%
Transport, storage and communication	3,6%	3,3%	3,4%
Public administration	6,2%	6,7%	7,7%

Education, health and social services	9,0%	8,7%	10,1%
Domestic services	6,3%	8,3%	8,2%
Other purposes	6,7%	7,6%	7,4%

Source: National Household Sample Survey (PNAD) (microdata) (2010)

The data in Table 3 also shows that in the last decade there has been a marked growth in industry in Paraíba, which may have been influenced by various factors, from political to technological advances in the countryside and in factories. Another important fact is the growth of MSEs compared to the number of companies in Paraíba and Brazil. In 2007, of the total number of active companies, 91.5 per cent in the state were classified as micro or small companies. This figure rose to 92 per cent in 2016, reaching a peak of 94.4 per cent in 2015. On the national scene, this figure increased by 0.9 per cent between 2007 and 2016, reaching 91.8 per cent of all active companies.

With the sharp increase in the number of companies on the market, competition is becoming ever more pronounced. The need to offer unique or differentiated products and services to increasingly demanding customers is no longer an optional feature, but essential for business survival.

However, research carried out to identify innovations in processes shows that the northeast is the region that invested the least in innovation between 2010 and 2012, where 54.1 per cent of respondents said they had introduced some new process or made significant improvements (SEBRAE, 2013, p 18). "Innovation is seen as the key to competing successfully in the global market" (SOUSA, 2006, p 16).

In this way, the lack of investment in innovation by small businesses in Paraíba jeopardises their competitiveness in other markets, taking time to adapt to new trends and improve their internal qualities, making them more resistant to fluctuations in the economy.

2.2. Quality philosophies and tools

2.2.1. A brief history of the evolution of quality

Over the course of four centuries, the means of manufacturing, of transforming raw materials into goods, have transformed and evolved at an accelerated rate compared to previous centuries. The revolution in the method of production, transforming predominantly artisanal manufacturing into a process of transformation on a large scale, was driven by technological advances, which made it possible to mechanise some production stations and to distribute products more quickly and efficiently.

This evolution in machinery technology, mechanising previously manual work, transformed products that were once unique and handmade into standardised and replicated products, thus making large-scale production possible, reducing the cost of production and the final price of products. In this way, the concept of quality underwent changes, as it was defined by the artisans according to the complexity and refinement of the production of that item, achieving full customer satisfaction (LINS, 2000). This transformation began to be standardised, with indicators and characteristics previously defined by entrepreneurs. At the end of the 18th century and throughout the 19th century, the first systems of industrial measurements and standards emerged, and quality inspection was implemented at the end of production.

In the 20th century, the concept of classical management and scientific management emerged with the work of Henry Fayol (1841 - 1925) and Frederick Winston Taylor (1856 - 1915). These works structured industry, dividing the functions and duties of each worker into sectors. They implemented the first time and motion studies, seeking to optimise productivity and reduce waste of labour and raw materials.

However, the theories of classical and scientific management demonstrate deficiencies in human resources, increasing the numbers of worker turnover, absenteeism, theft, sabotage and low productivity. In 1927, Elton Mayo (1880 - 1949) published an experiment known as the *"Hawthome Studies"*, in which he identified some factors that influenced the productivity of groups of workers in the electrical equipment sector at the *Western Electric* factory. This study made it possible to identify three factors that directly affect workers and their productivity: physiological, psychological and self-fulfilment.

In 1931, the statistician Walter Shewhart (1891 - 1967) presented a book called *"Economic Control of Quality Manufactured Products"*. This work introduced the concepts of Statistical Process Control (SPC), in which the worker responsible for operating the process would be able to control and monitor their own workstation, adjusting any non-conformities directly at the source. In addition to SPC, Water Shewhart also developed a quality management tool, in which he outlined a roadmap for continuous improvement. This tool became known as the PDCA cycle, where each letter stands for a stage, such as: *Plan (*P), *Do (*D), *Check (*C) and *Act (*A).

In the following decades, debates, studies and research in the field of quality continued to advance, and in 1950 Joseph M. Juran (1904 - 2008) published a set of his articles gathered in a book called *"Juran's Quality Handbook"*, which is considered an important quality engineering and management manual. The following year, Armand V. Feigenbaum (1922 - 2014) published a book entitled *"Total Quality Control"*, implementing a structure for quality throughout the organisation, no longer restricted to the manufacturing process, in order to maintain customer satisfaction and control industry costs.

At the same time, in 1950 there was a race to develop quality improvement programmes in Japanese industry. The development of quality in Japan, spearheaded by Kaoru Ishikawa (1915 - 1989), culminated in the emergence of new quality philosophies such as *Just-in-Time,* Six Sigma, 5S, SMED *(Single-Minute Change of Die)* and CCQ (Quality Control Circle). The philosophies implemented in Japanese production were one of the factors responsible for the upturn in industry, which after the destruction of the Second World War destroyed a large part of the factories and plunged Japan into a deep economic crisis, this upturn in the economy became known as the "Japanese miracle" (NISHIJIMA, 2012).

In 1982, physicist and statistician Wiston Edwards Deming (1900 - 1993) published a book entitled *"Out of the Crisis"*, in which he contradicted the principles of scientific management and placed the consumer as the most important part of the production line. He summarised his teachings in 14 points, in which he noted the importance of quality in the production process and the need for constant improvement of employees and the production process. Three years before the publication of *Out of the Crisis,* an American scholar, Philip B. Crosby (1926 - 2001), had already published a book entitled *"Quality is Free",* launching a philosophy of 0% defects, which became known by the phrase *"right first time"*. He argued that in order to produce without defects, it essentially depends on the management of the company's human resources, where the manager must create a collective awareness of quality (GOMES, 2004).

According to Falconi (2004) "[...] a quality product or service is one that meets the customer's needs perfectly, reliably, affordably, safely and on time". Therefore, for products and services to have these characteristics, the production process of which they are a part must also have quality, offering low-cost production, in an adequate time, without defects and perfectly meeting the product or service design.

2.2.2. Use of quality philosophies and tools

The term quality philosophy in this report should be understood as a set of ideas and attitudes aimed at achieving quality-related objectives. As such, quality philosophies guide corporate strategy in relation to internal resources. However, it is worth emphasising that quality tool should be understood in this report as a working methodology aimed at achieving a specific objective.

After defining quality philosophies and tools, this section will present case studies demonstrating the use of some quality philosophies and tools in different companies in Brazil and around the world.

2.2.2.1. Using the Six Sigma philosophy in an auto parts industry

Six Sigma is a set of practices developed by the Motorola company with the aim of systematically improving the production process and eliminating defects in both the process and the product. But with the diversification of the Six Sigma philosophy, various authors define it differently. According to Santos (2006):

> Six Sigma is an approach that drives the improvement of business performance and the enhancement of customer satisfaction, through a strategic management approach; the application of statistical thinking at all levels of activity; the use of performance indicators; the use of a systematised methodology that integrates a variety of techniques to evaluate and optimise processes; and the learning that results from the training and commitment of people.

Therefore, the Six Sigma philosophy requires people who are trained to manage it. These people have certifications known as *Green Belt, Black Belt* and *Master Black Belt.* These certifications define the professional's level of knowledge and preparation to manage or implement a Six Sigma system.

A case study was carried out in the auto parts industry, TTFix, which has 550 employees, spread over two manufacturing plants, with a turnover of US$ 35 million. The company is responsible for supplying auto parts to major car manufacturers such as Ford®, GM®, Fiat®, Honda®, Volkswagen® and others. Its mission was to become the largest supplier of fastening system solutions. However, improvements had to be made to the company's organisation, as well as cutting waste and increasing the quality of its products. The company therefore invested in implementing the Six Sigma philosophy, bringing about managerial, strategic and behavioural changes over the course of three years. These changes resulted in a financial gain of US$ 600,000.00 (six hundred thousand dollars), a 70 per cent improvement in the production process, greater operational control of the company, and the training of qualified professionals to manage the company (SANTOS, A.; MARTINS, M., 2010, p 46).

2.2.2.2. Using Kanban in a small textile company

Kanban is a quality tool in the Japanese philosophy of *Just-in-time, with the* aim of creating a harmonious system between the flow of information and the control of quantities produced at all stages of production. According to (PIRES, 1995 apud PRADO; PEREIRA, 2006, p 10), "Companies that prioritise delivery performance and quality, have little variability in the volume and total of items produced, have great potential to take advantage of the Kanban control system". In this way, companies that have high variability in production, seasonal demands and are not suited to a pull production system will have a high probability of failure when implementing Kanban.

The Kanban system was applied in a small company called Fiação Sigma. The company already used other quality tools such as the PDCA cycle, 5S and 5W2H in its organisation. This was a key factor in implementing the Kanban system, as this tool requires a certain level of control and organisation to work effectively in the organisation.

The company Fiação Sigma saw the need to reduce the amount of raw materials and stock in process and increase its production. It therefore made stock markings, signalling stock levels and visually highlighting when to place an order. The authors of the Prado and Pereira (2006) case study point out that the spinning line was signposted, speeding up the movement of materials in process, eliminating stocks of materials in process, freeing up the plant and increasing production efficiency.

The authors of the study highlighted these improvements, but did not obtain data related to the increase in production. However, these improvements make it possible to have greater control over production, avoiding wasted time, an increase in the company's working capital due to the reduction in stocks and greater productivity if the company continues to use the Kanban system.

2.2.3. Quality philosophy and tools to support business strategy

In Brazil there are 19,359,585 active companies (IBPT, 2016) competing with each other, seeking a larger share of the market or to maintain their survival in this competitive environment. The factors that determine their survival are diverse and may or may not have a positive influence, depending on the choices made by managers. Wright, Kroll and Pamell (2010, p. 29) make a comparison between companies and Charles Darwin's theory of evolution, where the company (animal) interacts with changes in the market (environment), and competes for customers (food) with other companies, and in order to maintain its ability to operate it must continually develop (evolve). Other authors question this analogy, as it doesn't fully portray the market, because in nature each animal evolves differently and various other factors influence this process, which doesn't fit the market.

However, some concepts can be extracted from this theory of evolution and revolution. One of them is improvement, where in order to carry out certain actions the company must have the necessary resources. In this way, organisational resources must be aligned with the company's objectives and mission, enabling the execution and fulfilment of pre-determined objectives. Being aware of the company's capacity, aligning goals with organisational resources and controlling external threats are key factors in business management.

In 1960 and 1970, two *Harvard Business School* professors, Kenneth Andrews and Roland Christensen, developed a tool called *SWOT* analysis, where S *(Strengths)*, W *(Weaknesses)*, O *(Opportunities)* and T *(Threats)*. This tool has become widely used in strategic planning, defining the company's path. This makes it clear how important it is to strengthen the company internally in order to resist external threats and take advantage of opportunities.

As discussed in section 2.2.1, it can be seen that quality philosophies and tools have contributed to the development of industry and service companies. They have enabled managers to organise their organisational resources more efficiently, making their businesses more profitable and enabling them to make greater progress and reduce the risk of bankruptcy. Quality philosophies and tools support strategic planning, building stronger foundations to resist external market forces, controlling resources, maintaining order and outlining paths through work methodologies.

According to Hisrich, Peters and Shepherd (2009 apud MINELLO; ALVEZ; SCHERER, 2012, p. 4) "Business failure occurs when there is a drop in revenue and/or an increase in expenses of large proportions, rendering the company insolvent and limiting the possibility of attracting debt financing or net worth". Following this logic, there are two ways to avoid business failure: increasing revenue and decreasing expenses. Therefore, the way in which the manager defines his strategies for achieving greater resources and cutting expenses will have an impact on the company's survival. There are some philosophies and tools that can help managers, as shown in Table 2.

It can be seen that the quality philosophies and tools presented in table 2 have a direct or indirect influence on the company's revenue and costs, many of which minimise the use of resources, increasing productivity, and improve the quality of the process and products, making it possible to increase market share.

Chart 2: Quality philosophies and tools

Philosophies and tools	Objective	Description
Six Sigma	Control process variability.	Monitors the production system, controlling non-conformities and systematically improving efficiency.
Lean Manufacturing	Minimise waste of resources.	It creates a methodology for continuous improvement in the use of productive resources, minimising losses.
Just-in-Time	Create a pull production system, which aims to zero out stock levels.	It creates a working methodology where resources are bought and used only when there are orders.
Kanban	Create a signalling system for production.	Create a demand signalling system using cards that are easy to see and interpret.
PDCA cycle	Continuous improvement	Quality tool that creates a methodology improving tasks, assisting in the planning, execution, checking and standardisation.
SMED	Minimise *setup* time.	Methodology for continuous improvement of *setup* times, minimising machine downtime.
Brainstorm	Generate new ideas	A working methodology that encourages a group to generate ideas for a specific objective.

2.3. Implications of Quality Philosophies and Tools

The application of quality philosophies and tools generates changes within the company, which can bring benefits to the organisation, production system and administration, but can also generate negative results, which can compromise an entire administration and generate a major financial and organisational collapse.

Using a tool or applying a quality philosophy without knowing its implications will result in unexpected results that could be positive or negative. A number of studies are needed to implement any change within the company, aligning the expected results with the strategic planning, knowing the positive and negative points, knowing the context in which the company is inserted, the behaviour of the employees, are some of the points to be checked and analysed before implementing any change.

Due to the importance of this knowledge, the most recent revision of ABNT NBR ISO 9001: 2015 incorporates new aspects into its standard that directly influence the quality management system.

In this way, this section will address the positive and negative points of some quality philosophies and tools, as well as the new ISO 9001: 2015 guidelines and their evolution, and some case studies showing the implementations and the consequences for the company.

2.3.1. New aspects of ABNT NBR ISO 9001: 2015

"ABNT NBR ISO 9001 was created in 1987 as a set of standards called ISO 9000, which includes standards 9001, 9002 and 9003 that define the requirements for putting a quality management system into effect" (ABNT NBR ISO 9001, 2015). When analysing the evolution of the requirements for implementing a quality management system (QMS) in manufacturing and service companies.

The first revision of ISO 9000 was carried out in 1994 without any major changes. However, after the revision in 2000, the three standards (9001, 9002 and 9003) were condensed into one standard, ABNT NBR ISO 9000:2000, which now consists of standards 9000, 9001 and 9004. This change made it possible to correct errors, allowing for a more simplified understanding and inserting new quality requirements focussed on the customer. Other revisions were made in 2005 and 2008, which sought to standardise the service of consultants, advisors, trainers and quality auditors in order to obtain ISO 9000 certification, as well as inserting environmental protection requirements.

The most recent revision took place in 2015, where a more comprehensive view was incorporated, allowing the analysis of various factors that now take into account the context in which the company is inserted, providing guidelines for understanding the organisation's needs, determining the scope of the QMS (Quality Management System).

Another approach added to the standard's requirements was risk management, which exposes to the manager certain attitudes that can cause damage to the QMS. This new revision takes into account another aspect that is uncommon in technical standardisations, the issue of leadership in the QMS, bringing senior management closer together and making them responsible for motivating the whole company and making quality management work.

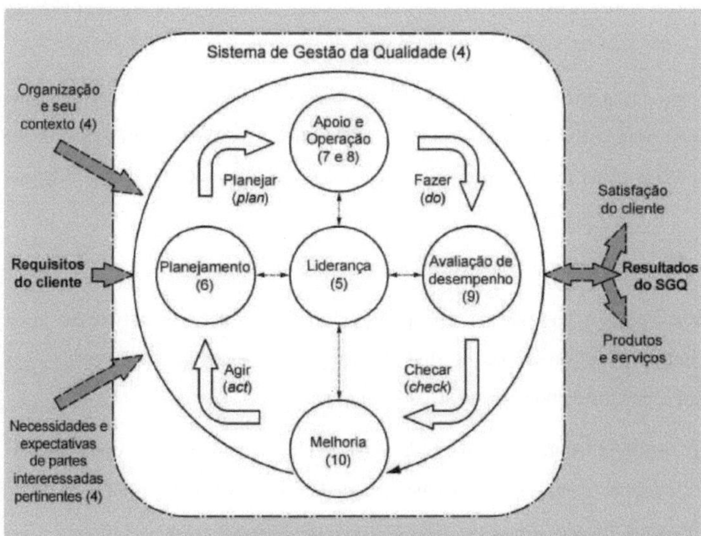

Figura 1:   ISO 9001:2015 Quality Management System

Source: ABNT NBR ISO 9001:2015 - Quality management system - Requirements Note: The numbers in brackets refer to the sections of the standard.

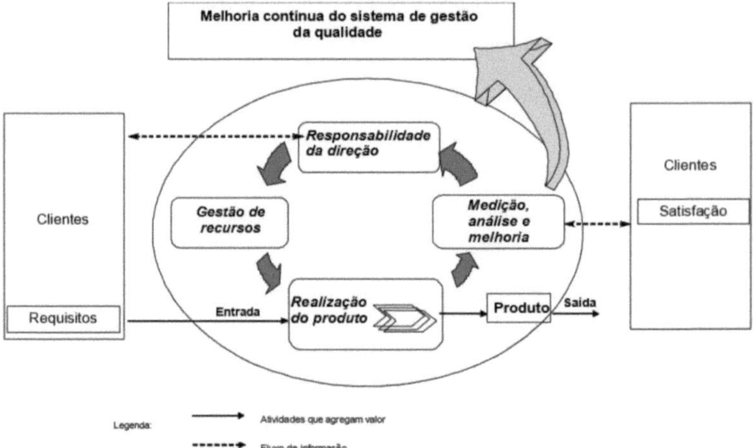

Figura 2:   ISO 9001:2008 Quality Management System

Source: ABNT NBR ISO 9001:2008 - Quality management system - Requirements

The ISO 9001 quality management system is based on the PDCA cycle, defining a system of continuous improvement. Figures 1 and 2 show the requirements for implementing the QMS in the 2015 and 2008 versions of the same standard. It can be seen that in 2015 issues such as leadership, the organisation's context and the needs and expectations of interested parties were included in the PDCA cycle.

In the 2008 edition, issues related to leadership, the context of the organisation, and the needs and expectations of interested parties were not explicitly addressed in the QMS, taking these points as something subjective to the perception and will of the manager, which he could do or not.

These issues were introduced in the new edition due to their importance in the QMS, and after observing that some companies were unable to adapt or maintain a QMS following the standards given in the 2008 edition. The new edition now better reflects reality, allowing a more flexible standard for each company to adapt to.

2.3.2.   Positive and negative points of quality philosophies and tools

The number of tools and philosophies that aim to improve production or service quality is unknown, because every day new companies, organisations or studies emerge with some kind of model, work methodology, philosophy and action instructions aimed at solving problems.

According to CAMPOS (2004) "A problem is the undesirable result of a process", thus, combining the concepts of quality with the guidelines of strategic management, a problem arises when the result of an action is not within the company's strategic planning, or results that do not contribute to achieving the pre-established goals and objectives. Thus, quality tools and philosophies have their own specific characteristics and can generate positive or negative results, depending on the type of problem to be solved.

20

Knowledge of the actions to be taken is fundamental to realising the objective you want to achieve, otherwise the risk of not obtaining the desired result will increase, thus creating a problem or an unwanted result. Each quality tool and philosophy has its own specific characteristics, i.e. each has its own specific objectives and cannot be applied generically.

Table 3 shows examples of the advantages and disadvantages of some quality-orientated methodologies and work philosophies.

Chart 3: Positive and negative points of quality tools and philosophy

Tool or Philosophy	Positive points	Negative points
Just-in-Time	- Low stock costs - Reduced *lead time* - Decrease in delays - Greater demand predictability	- Reduced product portfolio - Sensitive to market fluctuations - Low flexibility
6 Sigma	- Lower production costs - Control of the production process - Continuous improvement - Customer satisfaction	- High complexity Few trained professionals on the market High cost of implementation - High risk of implementation failure
Lean Manufacturing	- Agile processing - Reduced *lead time* - Cost reduction - Greater compliance - Greater flexibility - Low stock levels	- Engagement of all employees High implementation cost - Sensitive to supplier delays - Sensitive to unexpected demands
Kanban	- Reduction of materials in process - Reduced *lead time* - Stock control - Increased working capital	- Pull production system required - Sensitive to changing demands - Commitment from all employees
PDCA cycle	- Establishes a cycle of continuous improvement - Increases the likelihood of solving the problem - Efficient management of planned actions	- It takes a long time to prepare and planning - Does not apply to problems that require rapid action - It depends on the work and trust of the whole team
SMED	- Reduced *setup* - Increased equipment efficiency - Increased productivity	- Replacing resources - Duplication of resources - May require high equipment costs
Brainstorm	- Stimulates creativity - Helps generate products, solutions to problems - Helps with planning	- It takes a long time to evaluate each idea - There's no certainty that the idea will work Podegerar embarrassment among employees

Table 3 shows that some tools and philosophies have unique and similar characteristics. Having in-depth knowledge of their particularities is essential for successful implementation, as each one has limitations that can hinder the objectives set by the company.

2.3.3. Case studies

This section will use two case studies from the available literature to illustrate the implications of using quality practices in manufacturing companies, demonstrating the main changes within organisations and their consequences. The stages in the implementation of quality programmes will not be covered.

2.3.3.1. Implementing the 5S programme in a large company: importance and difficulties[1]

The 5S methodology was created by quality engineer Kaoru Ishikawa (1915 - 1989) in May 1950. The name 5S refers to the 5 concepts covered by this methodology in Japanese, which are: *Seiri* (utilisation), *Seiton* (tidiness), *Seiso* (cleanliness), *Seiketsu* (hygiene), *Shitsuke* (discipline). According to GEORGE et al (2005) "this methodology has the function of maintaining an organised, clean, safe and high-performance work environment".

This methodology was applied in a large company by another company specialising in implementing the 5S programme. This methodology requires the involvement of all employees, so the first change made in the company was to train and raise awareness among all the company's employees, from top management to shop floor workers. In order to disseminate this knowledge and guarantee the success of the programme's implementation, groups were set up to coordinate the gradual application of the 5S tool in each sector of the company. The company invested in more in-depth training for the coordinators, and awards for the sectors that managed to apply any S. The deadline set for applying each S was 3 months. This investment led to a number of changes in the company over the course of implementation.

In the initial phase of the programme, there was employee resistance to the programme, leading to conflicts of interest within some sectors. Mistakes were made due to a lack of experience or knowledge of the 5S programme, as well as problems reconciling it with other quality programmes already in place in the company. However, by persisting in the use of the 5S tool, it was observed that employees began to adopt the programme in their routines, creating a more harmonious environment. There was greater employee involvement in the quality programmes, leading to an improvement in the production sector, making it possible to reduce storage and maintenance costs, as well as increasing productivity.

Thus, despite the initial problems generated in the company by the use of 5S, generating conflicts and costs for the company, after complete implementation, the results obtained by the company were positive.

2.3.3.2. Case study on the implementation of pull production in a plastic packaging company.[2]

A pull production system is defined by linking the flow of product demand at all stages of purchasing,

---

[1] Source: COSTA, R. B.; REIS, S. A.; ANDRADE, V. T. **Implementation of the 5S programme in a large company: importance and difficulties.** In: ENCONTRO NACIONAL DE ENG. DE PRODUÇÃO. 25, 2005, Porto Alegre. Proceedings... 2005, p 1319-1325.

[2] Source: LEAL, A. C.; MACHADO, L. F.; COSTA, V. M. **Case study of the implementation of pull production in a**

processing and selling. Thus, customer demand generates a demand for the company's logistics, which generates a demand for production, and generates a demand for the supplier. It starts to produce for sale rather than to stock, generating small stocks of end products, stabilising demand and controlling production costs. This type of production system is characteristic of the JIT *(Just-in-Time)* philosophy, where the main objective is to have all the materials in conformity, in the correct quantity, at the required time, in the right place, and at exactly the right time, allowing the company to operate without stocks and without waste.

In the study in question, a plastic bottle company located in the state of São Paulo decided to transform its operations into a pull production system, eliminating as much stock as possible and controlling the company's production system. The company produced high and low density polyethylene, polypropylene and PET (polyethylene terephthalate) bottles. All production was carried out independently of its customers' needs, as the company produced to stock and then sell its products. Adopting this new system required a complete analysis of product demands, production methods and the physical space of the plant.

After analysing these aspects, the company realised that it would have to create production islands, or production cells, to manufacture certain products with similar demands, and carry out a new stock arrangement, divided by product type, to allow visual control.

Another aspect observed in the analysis was the lead time of each sector, where it was found that the bottle blowing sector was causing a bottleneck in the production system. To minimise this deficiency, machinery was purchased, the batch size of products from one sector to another was reduced, and investment was made in reducing *setup,* using some quality tools and equipment to speed up machine adjustments. In terms of communication, we opted to use the Kanban system to help exchange information between the production cells.

These changes in the method of producing, stocking and analysing production led to major transformations within the company. Investments were needed in training and hiring employees, renegotiating with suppliers, negotiating with customers to establish new ordering and supply policies, buying machinery and reducing the number of customers. However, the results obtained by the company after successfully implementing a new production system were positive: production costs fell, productivity improved, inventories were reduced, production control and efficiency improved and a culture of continuous improvement was consolidated.

---

company of plastic packaging segment. In: INTERNATIONAL CONFERENCE ON INDUSTRIAL ENGINEERING AND OPERATIONS MANAGEMENT. 18,2012, Guimarães - Portugal. Proceedings... 2012, p ID88.1 -ID88.10. Translation by the author.

2.4. Barriers to implementing quality philosophies and tools

This section provides a bibliographical survey of the barriers to implementing new quality philosophies and tools. Initially, the barriers were separated into two aspects. These are: resistance to change, where the employee or company managers do not accept the proposed changes; structural aspects, which involve the company's physical resources, such as machinery, equipment, number of employees, physical space, available capital, etc.

2.4.1. Resistance to change

When analysing the barriers that prevent the successful implementation of new methodologies in organisations, a psychological analysis of the human being is necessary, as there is still no company or organisation controlled solely by machines. This analysis will focus on the aspect of resistance to change or adaptation to new practices and methodologies in the workplace.

Adopting a new work methodology can generate fear, distrust, insecurity, discomfort, discouragement, irritation and other feelings among those involved in the company. These feelings can become an obstacle to the process of implementing change, affecting everyone from the shop floor to senior management.

Several authors put resistance to change as a factor that hinders total quality management (LIU, 1998; BRAVER, 1995; MILLER and CANGEMI, 1993 apud HERNANDEZ and CALDAS, 2001), as well as other initiatives such as company modernisation and improvement policies. Due to the importance of this topic, various studies have been carried out in an attempt to create recipes to avoid or resolve resistance to change. However, these efforts have not been effective enough to create a universal methodology for managing resistance to change (HERNANDEZ and CALDAS, 2001).

After various studies into resistance to change, it is still not possible to state in a deterministic way where resistance to change comes from or how it appears in organisations. For Zander (1950), resistance to change is something natural, arising in the course of implementation, but Kotter (1995), in new studies, found that resistance to change was not something natural, and could be avoided by analysing the individual's mind.

By individualising the problem of resistance to change, it is necessary to observe the feelings that change causes in the individual. Sigmund Freud (1856 - 1939) defines resistance as a self-defence reaction. For Castilho and Campos (2007), the most common origins of resistance are:

- Fear of the future (human beings opt for the familiar)
- Refusal of the transition burden
- Accommodation to functional status
- Fear of the past
- Lack of willingness to give up existing benefits

-Awareness of the weaknesses of the proposed changes

These origins can be linked to various aspects, making it difficult to define the problem of resistance to change. According to Oliveira (2003), the aspects can be classified according to table 4. Due to the complexity of the various factors that can cause an individual's resistance to change, it is difficult to determine a course of action for each situation, because according to Hemandez and Caídas (2001), practices that can encourage or reduce resistance to one aspect can negatively influence other aspects and generate new resistance.

Table 4: Aspects of resistance to change

Logical aspects Rational and logical objections	• Personal interests • Time/Effort • Cost • Viability
Psychological aspects Emotional and psychological attitudes	• Fear of the unknown • Understanding/Tolerance • Lack of trust • Security
Sociological aspects Interests of groups of sociological factors	• Political coalitions • Social values • Parish vision • Interests/Colleagues

Source: OLIVEIRA, 2003

According to Hemandez and Caídas (2001), individual resistance to change is linked to seven stages, as shown in figure 3. Each stage is characterised by the processing and perception of information relevant to the change, which is influenced by the aspects analysed in table 4, among others. The author points out that there may be four possible responses to the stimulus of change, which will depend on the integration of information and tendencies towards action, or may already emerge in the initial response after the proposal is presented, influenced by their pre-established concepts in the face of the first information. Being aware of these characteristics gives the manager or change agent a greater chance of identifying where the problem of resistance lies. It is therefore the responsibility of managers to identify the reasons that are generating resistance to change, and to try to minimise this barrier, taking into account the context in which the company and the individual are inserted.

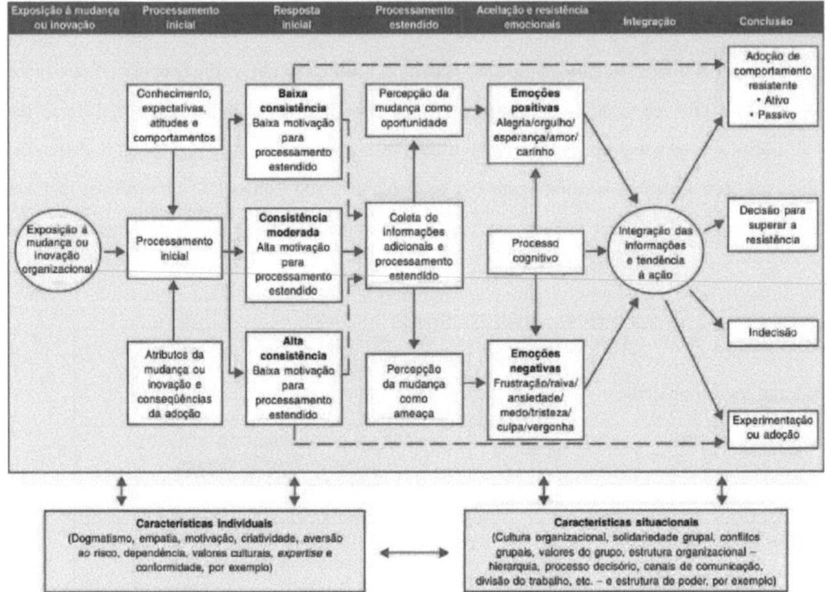

Figure 3: Model of individual resistance to change
Source: Hemandez and Caídas, 2001

The first stage of the model of individual resistance to change is exposure to the idea of change, where the individual becomes aware of the proposals for change. The second stage of the model reveals how the individual initially processes the new proposal, where they make a judgement based on their knowledge, expectations, the consequences of the change in their life and their individual characteristics. After this initial processing, the next stage refers to their response to the change, with low, moderate and high consistency of the change, where at this stage you can see people who already accept or deny the change. The extended processing stage is the point at which the people involved in the change will perceive the change, based on individual and situational characteristics, and judge whether the change is an opportunity or a threat. The next stage is characterised by the individual's emotional responses, which can be positive or negative. In the integration stage, all the information observed and felt by the individual will be integrated and then the person will assume their tendency to resist the change, overcome the resistance, remain undecided or try the change, in the conclusion stage.In the context of small companies, the complexity of identifying the cause of resistance to change is less when compared to larger companies. This aspect is characteristic of small companies, as analysed in section 2.1.2: having few employees, power being concentrated in the hands of a few or one person, the management sector being closer to the operational side, greater flexibility in the production sector, among other things, makes it easier to locate and reduce resistance to change on the part of those involved in the organisation.

2.4.2. Structural barriers

The implementation of quality tools and philosophies does not depend solely on the initiative of managers or workers; there are other structural limitations that could make the whole project unfeasible. Analysing the company's limitations is an essential factor in planning the organisation's strategic changes and actions (WRIGHT; KROLL; PARNELL, 2010). Implementing quality-oriented practices in business operations requires changes in work methodology, and knowing the limitations of the project and the organisation makes it possible to avoid project interruption, major damage and loss of productivity.

SWOT analysis is a widely used tool for checking a company's strengths, weaknesses, opportunities and threats when planning strategic business directions.

WRIGHT, KROLL AND PARNELL (2010) emphasise that a company's strengths and weaknesses constitute its resources. These include human resources (experience, skills, knowledge and abilities), organisational resources (the company's processing system, strategies, structure, culture, production, financial base, research, marketing and information system) and physical resources (facilities and equipment, geographical location, access to raw materials, distribution network and technology).

As mentioned in table 2, each tool and philosophy has its strengths and weaknesses, which can strengthen the company's resources, generating competitive advantage, or can weaken some strengths and make already weak resources weaker. In addition, the tools also require the solid structuring of certain resources in order for them to be viable.

According to CAMPOS (2004, p. 6), all internal productivity problems are solved with capital and knowledge. Disconnecting these two resources would make any improvement in productivity unfeasible.

So we narrowed down the structural barriers to implementing quality programmes to the internal environment, capital and knowledge.

However, there is an external context in which the company operates that can have a negative influence on the implementation of quality methods and systems. According to WRIGHT, KROLL AND PARNELL (2010), this external context is influenced by four different forces. These are

- Political-legal forces: refer to the outcome of elections, government programmes, taxes, incentives, legislation and court rulings;
- Economic forces: these include issues such as gross domestic product, interest rates, inflation, the value of the dollar and country risk;
- Technological forces: these are linked to scientific improvements and innovations;
- Social Forces: take into account the traditions, values, social trends and expectations that a society has of the company.

These external forces don't just depend on the capital and knowledge of an individual or organisation to be controlled. They are particularities that are independent of the company's management. However, the company can analyse and monitor the trend of these forces and prepare itself to withstand threatening scenarios.

However, for small companies, structural issues are relatively more difficult to control than for larger companies. This is due to the fact that small companies have limited capital for investments or safety reserves. Their income is low, and a significant portion of the profit is used as working capital to buy raw materials, equipment and machinery.

As various authors have pointed out (MINOZZI, 1987; GIMENEZ, 1988; GOLDE, 1986 apud BOAS, A. 2006, p 25), small companies flourish in scenarios where large companies have no interest, operating in different niche markets without having any control over events in the sector.

As a result, the ability to invest in change in small companies is limited due to the scarcity of capital. Consequently, the lack of capital prevents small entrepreneurs from having access to specialised people, consultants and skilled labour, increasing the barriers to implementing quality practices. However, CAMPOS (2004) warns that care must be taken to differentiate between the cause and effect of a problem. Lack of capital can be the result of bad management or waste in the production process, depleting capital reserves.

CHAPTER 3

METHODOLOGY

This chapter contains the methodology used in the research, the procedures carried out to obtain the data, and how the research was based.

2.5. Research methodology

The research began with a literature review on the subject. We used books, articles published in periodicals, master's and doctoral dissertations, and research carried out and publicised by public bodies such as SEBRAE, IPEA, IBGE and IBPT. Much of the material researched is available on the internet. In addition to gathering relevant data on the internet, informal interviews were held with teachers, civil servants, psychologists and businesspeople in order to outline the topics relevant to the research theme and understand the real problem regarding the use of quality tools and philosophies.

In the first stage of the research, an attempt was made to identify the economic situation of small businesses in Brazil and Paraíba, characterising their main economic aspects, as well as how they are structured. Informal conversations were held with businesspeople from Campina Grande, Sapé and João Pessoa, as well as ex-entrepreneurs of micro and small businesses, and the Institute of Micro and Small Businesses and surveys published by SEBRAE and IPEA were consulted. In this way, it was possible to outline the context in which small businesses operate, identifying their main limitations and advantages in relation to larger companies.

The second stage of the research focused on understanding the tools and philosophies of quality, not just the best-known ones, but in a general context. The research sought to carry out a historical survey of the development of quality programmes, to analyse the evolution of the ISO 9001 standard, with the aim of analysing its limitations, in order to verify that quality programmes have both positive and negative points. In addition to analysing the ISO 9001 standardisation, the research also checked case studies taken from journal articles available on the Internet, identifying the procedures for implementing practices aimed at operational quality, as well as the implications that these practices have had on the company.

The third stage prioritised understanding the barriers related to implementing new work methodologies, including quality tools and philosophies. Research was carried out into the bibliography available in books, articles and dissertations. Informal interviews were also conducted with psychologists working in the field of work organisation, with the aim of identifying aspects of human resistance to change.

Finally, formal interviews were carried out with four small business entrepreneurs, regardless of the company's line of business, following SEBRAE's classification by the number of employees, in the city of

Campina Grande, where a questionnaire (Appendix I) was drawn up based on SEBRAE's research entitled "Innovation in Small Businesses" in 2013, and another research carried out by Dextra consultancy, entitled "The Management of Organisational Change in Brazil" in 2013, as well as visits made to the businesses in order to observe the company's production system.

The aim of the questionnaire was to survey entrepreneurs about the structure of their company, their innovation practices and vision, the implementation of quality programmes, the difficulties and barriers they face in implementing programmes, access to information and the relationship between small businesses and public bodies.

2.6. Research limitations

The limitations of the research can be categorised into three aspects. Financial, accessibility to entrepreneurs and time.

As for capital, the research did not have the necessary funds to travel around Paraíba and/or other states, limiting its sample to the city of Campina Grande.

With regard to access to information, a total of 10 companies were consulted, but only 4 were willing to answer the questionnaire. In terms of time, the research didn't have enough time to carry out the implementation of quality programmes in small companies, in order to observe the implications and barriers present in the process. The research was therefore limited to carrying out a questionnaire to gather information and data from managers' experiences.

CHAPTER 4

RESULTS AND DISCUSSIONS

The results presented in this chapter will be divided into sub-chapters referring to the companies that were studied in this research, which will address the following characteristics. Organisational structure, practices and vision of innovation in quality programmes, access to information relevant to the company and barriers identified to the application of new quality philosophies and tools and their implications.

The section that introduces each company will address relevant questions about the company's structure, such as the command structure, number of employees, years in business, market niche and the company's main problem as identified by the interviewee; vision and innovation practices in quality programmes, such as their understanding of quality programmes and the importance the manager attaches to these practices; their ease of access to information relevant to their company, their knowledge of information sources and institutions that can help them; barriers and implications of quality tools and philosophies in their company.

All the data presented in this chapter was obtained through interviews with the founders or presidents of four small companies in the city of Campina Grande, following a questionnaire (Appendix I) drawn up by the author. The companies will be referred to as company α, company β, company γ and company δ.

2.7. Company a
2.7.1. Organisational structure

Company α has been in the plastic packaging business for five years. It currently has 23 employees working a single shift, from 7am to 5pm. Production is characterised by pull production, but the company keeps stocks of finished products to supply customers who make small purchases. Company a is run by a company made up of four brothers, where the founder is the father of the four brothers. Each brother owns 25% of the business, but only three actually work in the company, divided into the positions of president, production manager and sales manager. The interviewee signalled that he doesn't trust unknown people running his business.

The company has indicated that one of its biggest problems is the low working capital available, and that it is difficult to obtain financing from public banks, while borrowing from private banks is not worthwhile because of the high interest rates.

2.7.2. Vision and innovation practices in quality programmes

The interviewee from company A said that "innovation is the fuel to keep a company running", and in another question the interviewee gave a score of 10, on a scale of 0 to 10, for the importance of innovation in the company. The company therefore invests in product innovation, market research and maintains a close relationship with its customers, understanding their demands and trying to meet them.

However, the innovations carried out at the company are more restricted to the product and marketing, without making changes to the work methodology or inserting a new quality philosophy into the manufacture of its products. According to the company's chairman, the quality tools that are used are more closely linked to management. When asked which tool was used, the interviewee said that it was his own methodology and that it was part of the company's strategy, which he couldn't describe in the interview.

It can be seen that the company is aware of the importance of innovation and the use of tools and methodologies aimed at the quality of the company's operations. However, the manager does not invest in new work methodologies or the use of control tools.

2.7.3. Access to relevant company information

As far as access to information is concerned, the interviewee says that it is not difficult to have access to relevant content for his company, what is difficult is knowing how to filter the large amount of information and when to use it. Continuing on the theme, the interviewee says that the internet is a great source for researching solutions to various problems, and that in addition to the internet there are magazines, fairs and books that promote knowledge and access to necessary information. In order to stay informed and up-to-date, the interviewee says that he invests in the training of the company's managers, taking part in specialisation programmes. When asked what score the manager would give, on a scale of 0 to 10, for the ease of access to relevant information for his company, he gave a score of 6, dividing it by the lack of time to filter the huge amount of information. As for private and public institutions that can contribute to the company, the interviewee said that he knows SEBRAE, FIEP and other institutions, but he couldn't remember the names of the consultancies at the time of the interview.

When asked about the proximity of higher education institutions to small businesses, and whether this proximity should increase, the interviewee pointed out that the proximity of the university was fundamental to strengthening the company, because the university could contribute a lot to the development of all companies, but unfortunately this doesn't happen.

2.7.4. Barriers and implications of new quality philosophies and tools

Company A had some barriers when it came to applying quality programmes, whether it was the use of tools or new work philosophies. These barriers stem from a lack of knowledge of the quality management system, the tools and philosophies available and how to apply them. Another factor that causes barriers is the excessive duties of managers and the lack of a qualified production control professional. These two factors can make changes to the work methodology unfeasible, as not having knowledge of the relevant aspects of the programmes that are planned to be applied and someone who can dedicate themselves to these changes, managing the stages of the changes, means that the implementation runs a great risk of bringing more harm than good.

Financial issues make it impossible to implement quality programmes that require a high level of investment, but there are a large number of quality programmes that do not require a high level of capital investment. In this way, capital would be a secondary problem. With regard to resistance to change on the part of people in the company, there was no evidence that this was a problem.

The implications of implementing a tool or inserting a new quality philosophy in a company with characteristics similar to those presented, increases the likelihood of failure, bringing losses to the company, as the implementation hardly progresses beyond the superficial, since there is no notable knowledge of what is being applied or someone dedicated to the task of managing the change.

2.8. Company β
2.8.1. Organisational structure

Company β has been in the cleaning products manufacturing business for 9 years. The company has 20 employees who work the day shift. Production is characterised by a push system, as the company produces for stock before making sales. Company β is made up of just one owner, where it is managed by the founder and his wife, characterising it as a family business. In this case, the company also concentrates decision-making power in a few people, where the founder and his wife manage the financial, operational, sales and product purchases.

The interviewee pointed out that his biggest problem in maintaining the company is the low level of working capital, because financial institutions charge high interest rates on loans, making it difficult to expand and invest in the company. According to the interviewee, the concentration of power in their hands occurs because there are no reliable people with the knowledge to apply these tools at an affordable price on the market.

2.8.2. Vision and innovation practices in quality programmes

The interviewee stated that innovation is essential for a company. He gave the importance of innovation a score of 8 on a scale of 0 to 10, showing that he is concerned with offering quality and innovative products to his customers. To achieve this, the company's founder says he invests in research to develop and improve his products. When asked about quality philosophies and tools, the entrepreneur reported that he had no knowledge of techniques and methodologies aimed at strengthening the production system.

As for changes to the production system, the interviewee said that he had made physical changes and changes to the work methodology to adapt to the requirements of ANVISA (National Health Surveillance Agency), which had brought various benefits, such as greater production control, lower waste rates and greater productivity.

Despite the positive experience of using a quality philosophy, the entrepreneur reports that he is afraid of making changes and being fined by ANVISA, and that he has no knowledge of any philosophy or tool that could benefit his production, nor how to implement it, because, from his experience, these issues are complicated and require notorious knowledge of the subject.

2.8.3. Access to relevant company information

The company reveals that obtaining relevant information that helps the production process or that is relevant to the company is difficult; the interviewee gave this question a score of 4. According to the entrepreneur, the sources of relevant information would be trade fairs, as it is easy to obtain information on machines, processes, research and contact with new suppliers. With regard to continuing to specialise, the interviewee said that he studies individually as problems arise, but that at the moment he doesn't take part in specialisation classes. As for institutions that can contribute to the company, both private and public, the entrepreneur only knows SEBRAE.

Regarding the proximity of the university and its importance for the company, the entrepreneur observes that public and private universities should get closer to small businesses, and that this would bring many benefits to the company.

2.8.4. Barriers and implications of new quality philosophies and tools

The barriers at company β are similar to those at company α, and the structural characteristics of the two companies are similar. However, in company β the concentration of decision-making power is greater, and the manager also revealed that lately he hasn't had time to update or specialise. Another factor that has become a barrier to the implementation of quality programmes is the manager's resistance to changing his work methodology, as he fears that control bodies could fine the company.

As for capital, the company also faces problems with working capital, which makes quality programmes that require high investment unfeasible. However, as mentioned earlier, capital is a secondary barrier that does not apply to all quality tools and philosophies.

When it came to adopting the quality philosophy adopted by ANVISA, the entrepreneur said that there were various difficulties, from the legislation to adapting to the new way of producing, and that these changes resulted in a drop in productivity at first, but after adapting, productivity improved and the production system became more organised.

However, these changes were imposed on the sector by ANVISA regulations, which, according to the interviewee, caused a number of adaptation problems. Applying a philosophy or a quality tool with the same structural characteristics as today can lead to all kinds of problems if there is no dedication to change and knowledge of what is being applied.

2.9. Company y

2.9.1. Organisational structure

Company γ has been in the rope business for 10 years. The organisation has 79 employees and only operates during the day, i.e. mornings and afternoons. Its production system is characterised by push production, because according to the manager there are few variations in the product, so by forecasting demand based on the average sales for the period it is possible to anticipate orders and be ready for demand when it arises. Company γ is managed by the company's chairman and founder, but the company's decision-making power is not only concentrated in his hands. There are other departments that are managed by his son and other employees who are not part of the founder's family, these departments are production, HR, finance, *marketing,* research and the presidency.

The interviewee pointed out that the company's biggest current problem is maintaining the motivation and collaboration of all employees, getting everyone to follow the company's rules and working methods. In the interviewee's opinion, this is due to the lack of people who know the right way to deal with employees, who know how to detect lies and how to reward them when necessary.

2.9.2. Vision and innovation practices in quality programmes

According to the interviewee, the company has a culture of development and research into reusing materials to make its products. When asked about innovation, the interviewee said that "innovation is the realisation of things that already existed, but weren't used", and gave innovation a score of 10.

The company is concerned with constantly evolving and strengthening its production process. It invests in research to reduce its raw material and processing costs, and uses the *Just-in-time* philosophy, which is still being implemented. However, the manager already points out that there have been clear benefits in terms of production control, lower costs, less waste, shorter *lead times and* more.

The manager said that changes always aim to improve and fulfil the company's objectives, but if they are not implemented correctly, without the necessary knowledge and equipment, they can bring more harm than good, which is why the company γ analyses every possible change and only applies it if it is proven that the changes will bring benefits.

2.9.3. Access to relevant company information

Company y invests in the innovation of its products and processes. For this to happen, the interviewee reveals that obtaining information is extremely essential for innovation to take place. Thus, according to the manager, having access to information is not difficult, as the ease of having access to thousands of pieces of content on the internet facilitates this process, but what is difficult is understanding and putting it into practice, i.e. knowing how to apply the information received, thus the interviewee gave a score of 7 for ease of access to important information for the company. The interviewee says that he is always looking to specialise in order to improve the company. The interviewee pointed out that the government can't help him with much outside of tax issues, but as for private institutions, the company invests in consultancies to implement its quality programmes.

With regard to the interaction between universities and small businesses, the interviewee says that there should be less bureaucracy and greater ease for universities to get closer to small businesses. He also points out that universities have laboratories and equipment that could be used for research for small businesses, and that small businesses could help students gain access to a wider field of research.

2.9.4. Barriers and implications of new quality philosophies and tools

Company γ has a more suitable organisational structure for implementing quality programmes and philosophies than the previous two companies, since it does not concentrate decision-making power in a few people, there are employees responsible for implementing and running existing and new quality programmes, and it also has the help of a consultancy specialising in the subject. According to the interviewee, the biggest barrier for the company is the adaptation of employees to new working methods, knowing how to deal with employees who resist change and knowing how to control and depend on consultants to implement and manage the quality programme.

With regard to the financial side of things, the interviewee said that the tax side of things doesn't create so many problems for the company, and that there are enough resources to invest in the quality area. In this way, the company can invest in quality programmes that require higher levels of capital.

With regard to the implications of quality programmes, the manager said that every innovation or change initially causes discomfort, as it requires time to adapt and this initially causes performance to drop, but after adaptation the results surpass the previous ones. In this way, the programmes already in place are still causing adaptation problems, but benefits are already being seen.

2.10. ô Company
2.10.1. Organisational structure

Company ô has been operating in the clothing manufacturing market for 27 years, with 98 employees working single shifts in the morning and afternoon. The manufacturing process is characterised by the push production system, where the entire collection for a season is produced and then an attempt is made to sell the products, before a demand forecast is made for the orders on hand and an average for the past period. The company's management structure is subdivided into sectors, such as finance, production, HR, marketing, projects and the presidency. All these sectors are in the line of command below the presidency, which is headed by the founder and his son, and the other sectors are at the same level. It can be seen that decision-making power is not just concentrated in the hands of one or two people, but extends to the other management sectors of the company.

The interviewee pointed out that his company's biggest problem is meeting production deadlines and targets. He said that he has never been able to deliver his products on time, and this causes him problems with lost sales, excess stock, lack of production control and lack of planning.

2.10.2. Vision and innovation practices in quality programmes

According to the founder, company 8 is one of the few companies in the north-east that makes fashion, so there is always product innovation. In order to keep up with fashion trends, the interviewee points out that he is always investing in buying equipment that enables him to make new types of clothes, so he invests in embroidery, screen printing, other types of print and sewing. According to the founder, without innovation his company will go bankrupt, because in the fashion industry, if you don't create, you're left behind, so his view of the importance of innovation was given a score of 9.

As for innovation in the production process, the interviewee says that he is always adjusting the layout, work methodology and observing processes that should be carried out by the company or outsourced. According to the founder, he doesn't have much knowledge of quality philosophies and tools, but he tries to hire qualified people to make production more efficient and organised.

In this way, the entrepreneur says that a good idea will always have space in the company, that he is always open to hearing proposals and testing them, as long as he sees the benefit that the idea will bring to the company.

2.10.3. Access to relevant company information

Being constantly up-to-date with relevant information on fashion trends, the culture of the population, suppliers and sellers, as stated by the interviewee from company 8. To this end, the company's founder reveals that he invests in making sure that his employees responsible for creating fashion projects are always present at national and international fairs, and that he listens to his customers and the opinion of his sales staff. As for the ease of access to relevant information for the company, the entrepreneur gave it a score of 4, because all relevant information for the company doesn't come for free, and finding such good information reliably and for free is not easy to achieve, he also points out that he doesn't know of any private or public institutions that can help him manage or implement improvement methodologies in his company.

However, the interviewee points out that universities should get closer to small companies, and that partnerships such as internships, research and other actions would bring benefits to the company and also to the students' training.

2.10.4. Barriers and implications of new quality philosophies and tools

The barriers present in company δ are related to resistance to change on the part of the employees and the manager. The manager mentioned that he makes the necessary changes within the company, without following any methodology, just following his tacit knowledge. There are employees within the company responsible for controlling and improving production, where some quality tools such as the ABC curve, visual management, SOP (Standard Operating Procedure) are being implemented, but they are often modified by the manager, hindering the use of the tool and increasing the resistance of the workers, because with a high variation in the methodology it generates distrust in the workers.

In terms of capital, the company has enough slack to invest in quality programmes, purchase equipment and machinery, and invest in employee training.

The consequences of applying quality tools are reflected in the organisation of operations, where it has already been possible to reduce *lead times,* control stock and production more effectively and reduce waste. Variations in the methodology for using the tools create confusion for employees, leaving them unsure of how to act and so they act at their own discretion, causing non-conformities in production, misalignment of strategies and damaging the company's organisational climate.

CHAPTER 5

FINAL CONSIDERATIONS

The aim of this study was to map out the main barriers and implications of using new quality tools and philosophies in small companies. In this way, during the course of the research, the complex problem of using new working methodologies was realised, together with the various factors that influence small companies. Through detailed analyses of case studies, observation of the evolution of ISO 9001, and observations and interviews with small business entrepreneurs, it became possible to survey the main barriers and implications present in small businesses with regard to quality practices.

The research found that the aspects related to resistance in small companies are not as relevant as in larger companies, because the number of people makes the process of clarifying and motivating change easier. The organisational structure of small companies makes them more flexible, making this barrier easier to overcome. However, it cannot be concluded that there is no resistance to change, as companies β, γ and δ showed signs of resistance from employees and managers.

Barriers related to internal company factors are quite evident in the companies analysed in this research. Lack of knowledge of the quality tool or philosophy, the accumulation of tasks by managers, indiscipline and lack of respect for the criteria established for implementing changes are the main barriers observed in the internal environment of this research. As for capital, this is not a major problem, given the variety of quality tools and philosophies that can be implemented without large capital outlays. It is up to the manager to align their strategies with the methodology that best suits the context of their company.

External forces have a great influence on small companies, since compared to larger companies, small companies separately don't have enough strength to influence external forces. However, small companies find it easier to adapt because of their flexible structure. However, it is not always possible to adapt quickly to changes in the market. Issues such as a lack of skilled labour, legislation, taxes, consultants and suppliers can create barriers to making changes in the company. The main barriers found in terms of external factors were the lack of qualified labour, the scarcity of consultancies and the lack of government support for small businesses, so that it was not possible for the companies studied to hire qualified people, to find a consultancy that could help them implement a new working methodology or to adapt to the standards required by law. SEBRAE, a government body responsible for supporting micro and small businesses, was only known to two companies, and its remit was completely unknown to the other companies studied. In this way, the difficulty of implementing quality practices increases since there is no knowledge or fiscal support to implement such practices.

The implications observed in the companies and case studies analysed in this research are mostly positive. However, it can be seen that quality tools, when their aspects are not analysed and the management of their application is overlooked, bring negative results for the company. An example of this is company 5, where the application of quality tools suffers from variations in application methodologies, causing confusion, mistrust and resistance on the part of employees. The implications come in many forms, with the main causes of negative effects being inability to apply the tool or philosophy, lack of knowledge of its aspects, and partial implementation. These causes generate various negative effects such as lower productivity, disorganisation of the production process, confusion in work methodology, a deteriorating organisational climate, increased stress levels, demotivation, loss of power of command, etc.

The observations made in the companies, combined with the vision of each entrepreneur and the support of studies related to the subject, make it possible to affirm that the main barriers present in small companies to the use of quality tools and philosophies is the lack of knowledge, which means that the installation of these quality programmes is unsuccessful, generating negative consequences for the small entrepreneur.

For future work, we recommend the application of quality tools and philosophies, as well as their monitoring, in small companies, in order to visualise in practice the barriers and implications that arise from the use of new working methodologies.

BIBLIOGRAPHICAL REFERENCES

ALBUQUERQUE, A. F. **Gestão estratégica das informações internas na pequena empresa: estudo comparativo de casos em empresas do setor de serviços (hoteleiro) da região de Brotas-SP.** 2004, 209f. Dissertation (Master's in Production Engineering). University of São Paulo, São Carlos, 2004.

ALVES, T. DE P. C. **Continuous improvement: importance and application in the production process of a metallurgical industry.** 2010, 54f. Final course work (Bachelor's Degree in Production Engineering) - Anhembi Morumbi University. São Paulo, 2010.

BRAZILIAN ASSOCIATION OF TECHNICAL STANDARDS. **ABNT NBR ISO 9001:2015:** ABNT NBR ISO 9001:2015. São Paulo: ABNT, 2015. Available at: <http://www.abntcatalogo.com.br/norma.aspx?ID=345041>. Accessed on: 08 May 2016.

BRAZILIAN ASSOCIATION OF TECHNICAL STANDARDS - ABNT. **Quality management system - Requirements:** ABNT NBR ISO 9001:2008. São Paulo, 2008.

UPDATE FROM ABNT NBR ISO 9001:2008 TO ABNT NBR ISO 9001:2015. São Paulo: **Brazilian Association of Technical Standards (ABNT),** 2015.

BALBÃO, M. S.; RIBEIRO, L. M.; ALLIPRANDINI, D. H. **Characterisation of the role of the production function in small-sized industries (SME) in the city of São Carlos: a case study.** In: NATIONAL PRODUCTION ENGINEERING MEETING - ENEGEP. 24, 2004, Florianópolis. Proceedings... 2004, p. 442-449.

NATIONAL DEVELOPMENT BANK - BNDS. **Who can be a client.** Available at < http://www.bndes.gov.br/wps/portal/site/home/financiamento/guia/quem-pode-ser-cliente >. Accessed on 30 July 2016.

BARBOSA, C. L.; LIMA JR, O. F. **Implications of implementing lean production system techniques in the supply chain of a precast concrete pile factory.** In: NATIONAL PRODUCTION ENGINEERING MEETING - ENEGEP. 31, 2011, Belo Horizonte. Proceedings... 2011, 12f.

BOAS, ANA A. V. **Fundamental guidelines for managing sustainable change in small businesses.** 2006, 141 f.

Dissertation (Master's Degree in Management Sciences and Business Strategy) - Federal Rural University of Rio de Janeiro, Seropédica, April 2006. Available at http://www.dominiopublico.gov.br/pesquisa/DetalheObraForm.do?select_action=&co_obra=65876 >. Accessed 1 September 2016.

BRAZIL. Constitution (1988). Constitution of the Federative Republic of Brazil. Brasília, DF: Senado Federal1988 . Disponívelem :< http://www.planalto.gov.br/ccivil_03/constituicao/constituicaocompilado.htm>. Accessed on 3 August 2016.

CAMPOS, VICENTE FALCONI. **TQC - total quality control (Japanese style).** 8. ed. Nova Lima - MG: INDG Tecnologia e Serviços Ltda, 2004. 256 p.

CASTILHO, J. H.; CAMPOS, R. R. The human factor and resistance to organisational change during the information system implementation phase: a case study in a technology implementation company. **Interface Tecnológica,** v. 4, n. 1, p. 118-127, 2007.

COSTA, R. B.; REIS, S. A.; ANDRADE, V. T. **Implementation of the 5S programme in a large company: importance and difficulties.** In: ENCONTRO NACIONAL DE ENG. DE PRODUÇÃO. 25,2005, Porto Alegre. Proceedings... 2005, p 1319-1325.

COSTA, SIMONE M.; MILLER, D. **The management of organisational change in Brazil.** Dextera Consultoria. 2013. Available at < http://www.mundopm.com.br/ed55/Artigo09_PesquisaDextera.pdf >. Accessed on 14 July 2016.

CROSBY, PHILIP B. **Quality is Investment.** Translation by Áurea Weissenberg. 7. ed. Rio de Janeiro: José Olympio, 1999, 327 p.

DALLA, W. D.; MORAIS, L. L. P. **Lean production: competitive advantages and disadvantages resulting from its implementation in different organisations.** In: SIMPÓSIO DE ENGENHARIA DE PRDOUÇÃO - SIMPEP. 13, 2006, Bauru. Proceedings... 2006, 1 If.

DARWIN, C. **The origin of species, in the midst of natural selection or the struggle for existence in nature.** 2003, v. 1, translated by Dr Mesquita Paul.

GEORGE, M. L et al. *The Lean Six Sigma pocket: toolbox. New York: The McGraw-Hill Companies,* 2005, 281 p.

GHOBRIL, A. N.; BANEDITTI, M. H.; FRAGOSO, N. D. **Innovative practices in the bar, restaurant and snack bar sector.** In: ENCOUNTER OF STUDIES IN ENTREPRENEURSHIP AND SMALL BUSINESS MANAGEMENT - EGEPE. 8, 2014, Goiânia. Proceedings... 2014, p 1-15.

GOMES, PAULO J. P. **The evolution of the concept of quality: from manufactured goods to information services.** Cadernos Bad, 2004, p. 6-18.

GONÇALVES, JOSÉ E. L. The need to reinvent companies. **RAE - Revista de Administração de Empresas.** São Paulo, v. 38, n. 2, p. 6-17, 1998. Available at < http://www.scielo.br/pdf/rae/v38n2/a02v38n2.pdf >. Accessed on 20 August 2016.

GONÇALVEZ, A.; KOPROWSKI, S. O. **Pequena empresa no Brasil.** São Paulo: Edusp, 1995.

HERNANDEZ, J. M. DA C.; CALDAS, M. P. Resistance to change: a critical review. **REA - Revista de Administração de Empresas,** v. 41, n. 2, p. 31-45, Apr./Jun. 2001.

BRAZILIAN INSTITUTE OF GEOGRAPHY AND STATISTICS - IBGE. Available at < http://www.ibge.gov.br/home/ >. Accessed on 29 July 2016

BRAZILIAN INSTITUTE OF GEOGRAPHY AND STATISTICS - IBGE. **National Household Sample Survey (PNAD).** 2010. Available at < http://www.ibge.gov.br/home/estatistica/pesquisas/pesquisa_resultados.php7id_pesquisaM0 >. Accessed on 5 August 2016.

BRAZILIAN INSTITUTE OF PLANNING AND TAXATION - IBPT. **Empresômetro MPE.** Available at: < http://empresometro.cnc.org.br/ >. Accessed on 29 July 2016.

APPLIED ECONOMIC RESEARCH INSTITUTE - IPEA. **Paraíba in the national, regional and internal context.** 80f. Text for discussion 1726, Rio de Janeiro, April 2012. Available at http://www.ipea.gov.br/portal/index.php?option=com_content&view=article&id=15454 >. Accessed on 3 August 2016.

INSTITUTE FOR APPLIED ECONOMIC RESEARCH - IPEA. **Micro and small enterprises: labour market and implications for development.** 232f. Rio de Janeiro, 2012.   Available at http://www.ipea.gov.br/agencia/images/stories/PDFs/livros/livros/livro_micro_pequenasempresas.pdf >. Accessed on 3 August 2016.

APPLIED ECONOMIC RESEARCH INSTITUTE - IPEA. **Projections of qualified labour in Brazil: an initial proposal with scenarios for the availability of engineers until 2020.**   56f. Text for discussion 1663, Brasília, September 2011.
                                        Available< http://www.ipea.gov.br/portal/index.php?option=com_content&view=article&id=1 0455 :td-1663-projections-of-skilled-labour-in-brazil-an-initial-proposal-with-scenarios-for-the-availability-of-engineers-up-to-2020&catid=170:2012&directory=l >. Accessed on 5 August 2016.

KOTTER, J. P. *Leading change: why transformation efforts fail.* **Harvard Business Review,** Boston, v. 73, n. 2, p. 59-67, mar. 1995.

, Complementary Law nª 147, of 07 August 2014. Amends Supplementary Law No. 123, of 14 December 2006, and Laws No. 5.889, of 8 June 1973, No. 11.101, of 9 February 2005, No. 9.099, of 26 September 1995, No. 11.598, of 3 December 2007, No. 8.934, of 18 November 1994, No. 10.406, of 10 January 2002, and No. 8.666, of 21 June 1993; and makes other   provisions.   Federal   **Official   Gazette,**   Brasília,   DF,   2014.   Available   at: < http://www.planalto.gov.br/ccivil_03/leis/LCP/Lcpl47.htm>. Accessed on 3 August 2016.

LEAL, A. C.; MACHADO, L. F.; COSTA, V. M. **Case study of the implementation of pull production in a company of plastic packaging segment.** In: INTERNATIONAL CONFERENCE ON INDUSTRIAL ENGINEERING AND OPERATIONS MANAGEMENT. 18, 2012, Guimarães - Portugal. Proceedings... 2012, p ID88.1 - ID88.

LINS, BERNARDO E. **Breve história da Engenharia da Qualidade.** Cadernos ASLEGIS, v. 4, n. 12, p. 53-65, Sep/Dec 2000.

MARTINS, P. P. P.; BIDIN, L. A. **M. O Sistema *Just in Time',* uma visão crítica de sua implementação.** In: SIMPÓSIO DE ENGENHARIA DE PRODUÇÃO - SIMPEP. 13, 2006, Bauru. Proceedings... 2006, 12f.

MINELLO, I. F.; ALVES, L. DA C.; SCHERER, L. A. **Business failure: a perspective from entrepreneurs who have experienced failure.** In: ENCONTRO DE ESTUDOS SOBRE EMPREENDEDORISMO E GESTÃO - EGEPE. 7, 2012, Florianópolis. Proceedings... 2012, 18f.

MOREIRA, S. F.; SOUZA, C. A. **Decision support systems in small and medium-sized enterprises: Comparative case studies in small commercial companies.** In: FEA-USP ADMINISTRATION SEMINARS - Semead. 7, 2004, São Paulo. Proceedings... 2004.

NISHUIMA, SHOJI. Japanese industrial policies. **Tempo do Mundo magazine,** v. 4, n. 3, p 75-96. 2012. Available at < http://repositorio.ipea.gov.br/bitstream/! 1058/6307/l/RTM_v4_n3_Politicas.pdf >. Accessed on 28 August 2016.

OLIVEIRA, A. F. **Evaluation of the impact of implementing a technological innovation on the external customers of a service company - the case of speech recognition technology in a telecommunications company in the state of Minas Gerais.** 2003. 140f. - Dissertation (Master's in Production Engineering). Federal University of Santa Catarina, Florianópolis, 2003.

OLIVEIRA, O. J. Small business in Brazil: a study of its characteristics and prospects. **Revista Integração,** ano 12, n. 44, p. 5-15, jan/feb/mar 2006.

PELISSARI, A. S. **Strategy formulation process in small companies based on corporate culture and managerial competences.** 2007, 22 If. Thesis (Doctorate in Production Engineering) - Faculty of Engineering, Architecture and Urbanism, Methodist University of Piracicaba - UNIMEP. Santa Bárbara D'Oeste, 2007.

PEREIRA JR. R. P. *Kanban-.* **use in industry, aiming to reduce costs by organising and controlling stocks.** 2003, 39f. Final course work (Bachelor's Degree in Accounting) - Federal University of Santa Catarina, Florianópolis, 2003.

PINHO, CARLOS T. A. **Six Sigma: A proposal for implementing the methodology in small and medium-sized companies.** 2005. 118 f. Dissertation (Master of Science in Production Engineering) - Federal University of Rio Grande do Norte, Natal, 2005.

PINTO, S. H. B.; CARVALHO, M. M.; HO, L. L. **Implementation of quality programmes: a** *survey of* **large companies in Brazil.** GESTÃO & PRODUÇÃO, v. 13, n. 2, p. 191-203, mai/ago 2006.

PRADO, M. C.; PEREIRA, M. Implementation of the *Kanban* system in a small textile company: a case study in the spinning sector. **RACRE - Revista de Administração,** v. 6, n. 10, p. 07- 15, jan./dez. 2006.

REZENDE, F. P.; FREITAS, F. O.; SILVA, E. A. T. DE O. **Organisational culture and resistance to change.** In: SYMPOSIUM OF EXCELLENCE IN MANAGEMENT AND TECHNOLOGY - SEGeT. 8, 2011, Resende-RJ. Proceedings... 2011,16f.

RODRIGUES, M. E. **O conhecimento nas micro e pequenas empresas: Um estudo sobre sua absorção e utilização nas micro e pequenas empresas fluminenses.** 2000, 158f. Dissertation (Master's in Administration) - Federal University of Rio de Janeiro, Rio de Janeiro, 2000.

RODRIGUES, J. T. M. C.; WERNER, L. **Describing the Six Sigma programme: a literature review.** In: NATIONAL PRODUCTION ENGINEERING MEETING - ENEGEP, 28,2008,   RiodeJaneiro   .
               Anais...2008 ,   15f   .
Available at < http://www.abepro.org.br/biblioteca/enegep2008_TN_STP_070_498_11368.pdf >. Accessed on 5 September 2016

ROSSI, D. U. et al. **Challenges in implementing a quality of life at work programme: a case study in a small chemical industry.** In: NATIONAL PRODUCTION ENGINEERING MEETING - ENEGEP, 31, 2011, Belo Horizonte. Proceedings... 2011,1 lf.

SANTOS, L. P. **Fundamental guidelines for managing sustainable change in small businesses.** 2006, 14lf. Dissertation (Master's Degree in Management Sciences and Business Strategy) - Federal Rural University of Rio de Janeiro, Seropédica, 2006.

SANTOS, A. B.; MARTINS, M. F. Contributions of Six Sigma: case studies in multinational companies. **Revista Produção,** v. 20, n. 1, p. 42-53, jan./mar. 2010.

SANTOS, MARCEL DE S. E S. **Management of organisational change: a theoretical review.** 2014, 106f. Dissertation (Master's in Business Management) - Getulio Vargas Foundation, Rio de Janeiro, 2014.

BRAZILIAN SUPPORT SERVICE FOR MICRO AND SMALL ENTERPRISES - SEBRAE. **Survival rate of companies in Brazil.** Studies and Research Collection, 30 f. October 2011.   Available at http://www.sebrae.com.br/Sebrae/Portal%20Sebrae/Anexos/Sobrevivencia_das_empresas_no_Brasil_ 201 l.pdf >. Accessed on 15 August 2016.

BRAZILIAN SUPPORT SERVICE FOR MICRO AND SMALL ENTERPRISES - SEBRAE. **Survival rate of companies in Brazil.** Studies and Research Collection, 72 f. 2013.   Available at http://www.sebrae.com.br/Sebrae/Portal%20Sebrae/Anexos/Sobrevivencia_das_empresas_no_BrasiU   2013.pdf   > Accessed on 15 August 2016.

BRAZILIAN SUPPORT SERVICE FOR MICRO AND SMALL ENTERPRISES - SEBRAE. **Survival rate of companies in Brazil.** Research Report, 40 pages, November 2004.   Available at http://www.wdigital.com.br/mba/estrategia/relatorio_pesquisa_mortalidade_minas.pdf >. Accessed on 01 August 2016.

BRAZILIAN SUPPORT SERVICE FOR MICRO AND SMALL ENTERPRISES - SEBRAE. **Innovation in Small Businesses.** Strategic Management Unit - UGE, 80f., December 2013.   Available at http://www.bibliotecas.sebrae.com.br/chronus/ARQUTVOS_CHRONUS/bds/bds.nsf/lb7ec4b5cd66b3 a2c39e64fa84c403fb/$File/5064.pdf >. Accessed on 2 August 2016.

BRAZILIAN SUPPORT SERVICE FOR MICRO AND SMALL ENTERPRISES - SEBRAE. **Participation of micro and small companies in the Brazilian economy.** Strategic Management Unit UGE,   108f., july2014   .
Available<
http://www.sebrae.com.br/Sebrae/Portal%20Sebrae/Estudos%20e%20Pesquisas/Participacao%20das %20micro%20and%20small%20companies.pdf >. Accessed on 27 July 2016.

BRAZILIAN SUPPORT SERVICE FOR MICRO AND SMALL ENTERPRISES - SEBRAE. **Survival of companies in Brazil.** Studies and Research Collection, 72 f., Brasília, 2013.   Available at http://www.sebrae.com.br/Sebrae/Portal%20Sebrae/Anexos/Sobrevivencia_das_empresas_no_BrasiU   2013.pdf   >. Accessed on 27 July 2016.

SOUSA, J. C. **Innovation in the organisational context: facilitating factors and hindering factors.** 2006, 187 f. Dissertation (Master's in Social Management and Labour) - University of Brasília, Brasília, 2006.

TELES, B. A. W.; AMORIM, M. R. L. Overcoming difficulties in implementing information systems in organisations. **Rev. de Administração da Faculdade Novo Milénio.** 2013,15f. v. 6, n. 1.

WRIGHT, P.; KROLL, M. L; PARNELL, J. **Strategic management: concepts.** Translated by Celso A. Rimoli, Lenita R. Esteves. 11. reimpr. São Paulo: Atlas, 2010,433 p.

ZANDER, A. F. *Resistance to change: its analysis andprevention.* **Advanced Management,** New York, v. 4, n. 5, p. 9-11, 1950.

APPENDIX I

Questionnaire used as a guide for interviews with small business owners

1. Education

2. How many employees are there in your company?

3. How many shifts does the company work?

4. How old is your business?

5. How is the company's organisation chart drawn up?

6. Is the company's production characterised as push or pull?

7. Do you know any quality tools and/or philosophies?

8. Before starting your business, were you familiar with any quality tools and/or philosophies?

9. Do you have a policy of collecting production data?

10. Have you made any changes to your company's organisation?

11. Who was responsible for managing these changes?

12. Is all the decision-making power in your company concentrated in your hands, or are other employees there to help you?

13. Have these changes brought benefits? Which ones?

14. Has the company faced any difficulties in making these changes? Such as:

     a. Workers' resistance
     b. Resistance from partners or managers
     c. Lack of knowledge in applying changes
     d. Lack of money
     e. Difficulty accessing new technologies
     f. Lack of skilled labour
     g. Lack of discipline to maintain changes
     h. Employee motivation
     i. others

15. What does innovation mean to you?

16. On a scale of 0 to 10, how would you rate the importance of innovation in your company?

17. On a scale of 0 to 10, how would you rate the ease of access to relevant information for your company?

18. On a scale of 0 to 10, how necessary is it for your business to make changes now?

19. On a scale of 0 to 10, how would you rate your ability to manage these changes?

20. Are you aware of any resources where you can search for information relevant to your company?

21. Do you continue to study or specialise?

22. In your opinion, should universities get closer to small producers?

23. Do you know of any government bodies or private consultancies that help organise your company?

24. What is the biggest difficulty your company faces or has faced in recent years?

25. What measure would have helped you face or have faced this difficulty?

Printed by Books on Demand GmbH, Norderstedt / Germany